H. journey. Brother Jaye

1.
ed
30, 17

MW00896497

Inescapable Quotes
with Inescapable Art© 2017 Brother Sage

No part of his book may be reproduced by any mechanical, photographic, or electronic process, or in the form of a phonographic recording, nor may it be stored in a retrieval system, or transmitted, or otherwise be copied for private or public use – other than for "fair use" without prior written permission of the publisher, author, and editor.

Inescapable Publications

Book was edited and arranged by Lori Emmons,
a friend of Brother Sage,
aspiring author, Holistic survivor of Multiple Sclerosis.
info@emmonslori.com

DEDICATION

These Inescapable Quotes and Artwork are dedicated to the Infinite Source of Inspiration that, I AM, in us all.

May everyone who breathes in deeply the words on every page be ridiculously blessed with Wisdom, calmness of mind, evolution in Consciousness, Joy in Spirit and a shift in Perception contained in these treasures.

Received and transcribed by Brother Sage

Forward by Leila Sun

One of the quickest ways to release, shift and

bring joy back into one's life is through laughter.

Brother Sage is a spirited, magical, and delightful,

channel of inspirational quotes which immediately

reconnect you to Spirit and remind of you of your

natural state of Divinity. He does this in a simple,

yet deeply contemplative, humorous, and loving way.

Ready to take a quantum leap in consciousness

with a smile, twinkle back in your eye and remember

the powerful co-creator you are on the planet?

Take a deep breath and take in every one of

Brother Sage's Inescapable Quotes.

As Brother Sage would say - "You're Worth It!"

Transformational Lyme Disease Coach, Leila Sun,
www.LeilaSun.com

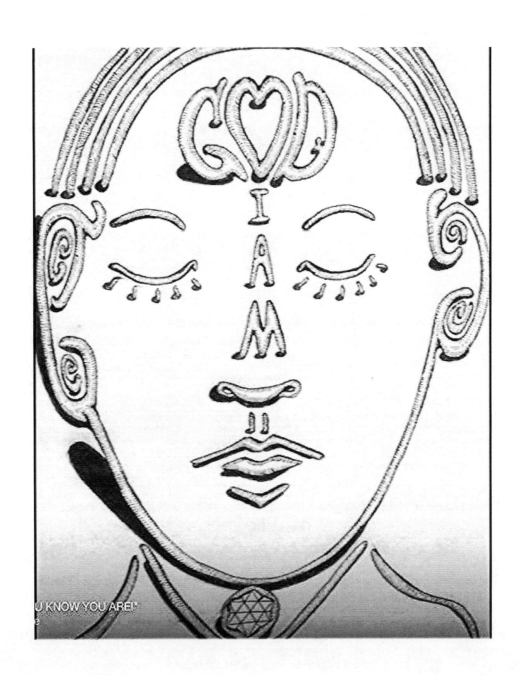

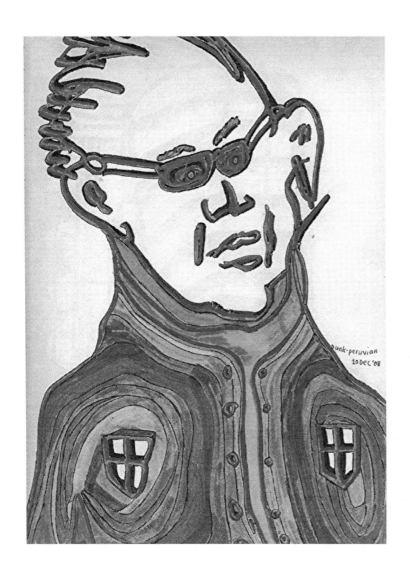

"It is no longer I who lives, but I AM who lives through me."

Our hearts speak to all hearts in a language beyond intellect. Why go anywhere else to understand reality?
Brother Sage

"Your heart and breath have the innate power to save you from your mind. Let your heart flower with this Breath."

in the name
of The Light,
  I give thanks + pray
        7.30.3
        Sage

12

"Attention received from suffering: some get off on it instead of getting off of it."

"Love is the ultimate "spot" remover."

Inescapable Love, is Love.
Invite your beloved Love in your
heart to stay.

Brother Sage

"If you can't be with the food you love, then love the food you're with."
(c) 2017 Brother Sage

Cowfish

Love was built into all of creation. If you don't see it, look again.

"The final frontier is to return home to loving, appreciating, honoring, and respecting yourself."

I am an ambassador
of inescapable joy.

Brothersage.com

"There are more people sending love, blessings & prayers to all beings than you realize."

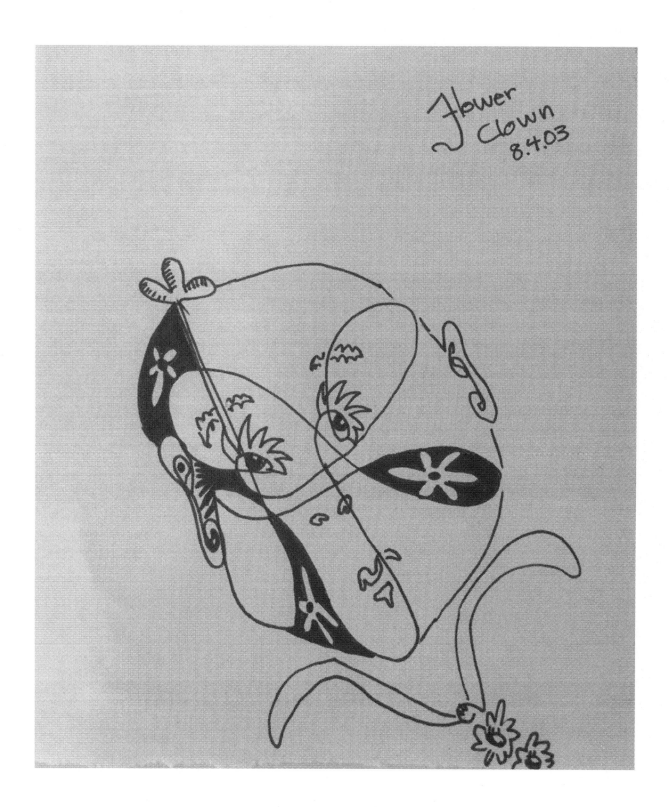

Flower
Clown
8.4.03

"The greatest confidence or honor goes to The Divine Presence within."

COSMIC EGG
11 FEB 1950

"Is love flowing abundantly in your life and world today?"

"I bow repeatedly to the Primal One.
To the one without form.
To the one without color.
To the one without sound or beyond sound
or the unstuck sound.
Throughout the ages, you are the one and
same."

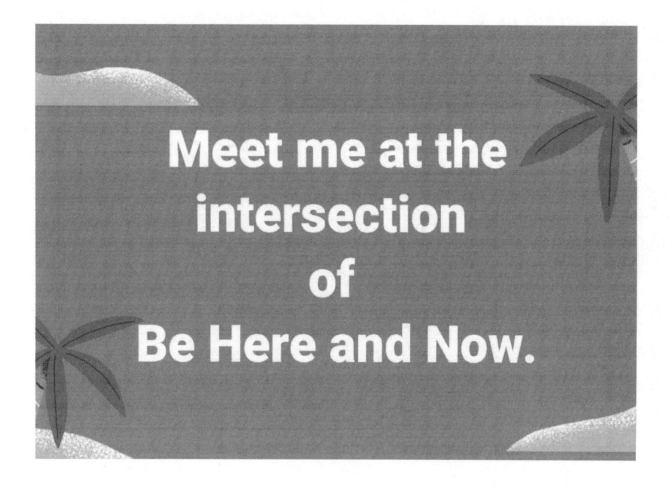

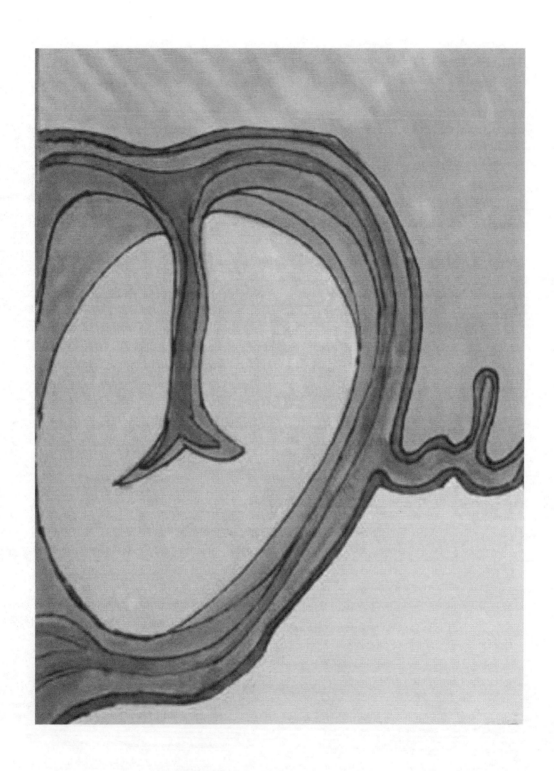

"What is beyond measure cannot be measured. Such is Love."

QUESTION THE REALITY OF THE WORLD YOU ARE PRESENTED. KNOW THYSELF & BE FREE.

BrotherSage.com

"Get the immortality upgrade, your body/mind it's getting younger and healthier."

"Sacred = Everything that we honor and respect.
Start with yourself."

"Here, I AM
Here, I AM perfection
Here, I AM harmony
Here, I AM joy
Here, I AM health."

"Simple… Feel every moment and let the heart do the speaking."

"Let this next breath bring forth God's Light and Grace. May I be a blessing and of service to all Beings this day."

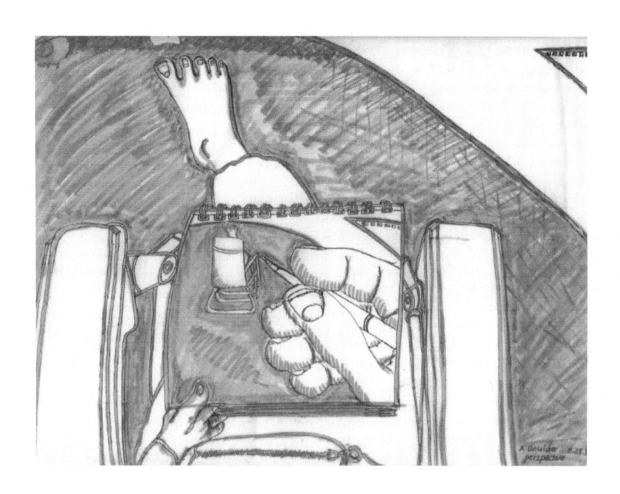

"I see you. Do you see you?
You're amazing!!"

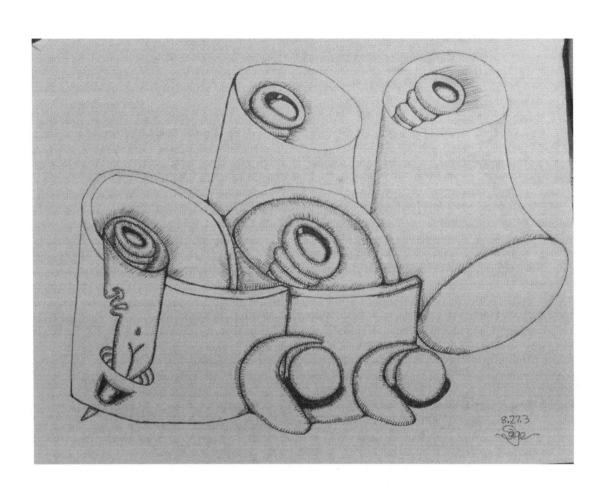

"Gratitude is the attitude that Raises you to a higher Latitude."

"May you be able to withstand the grace of your endless blessings."

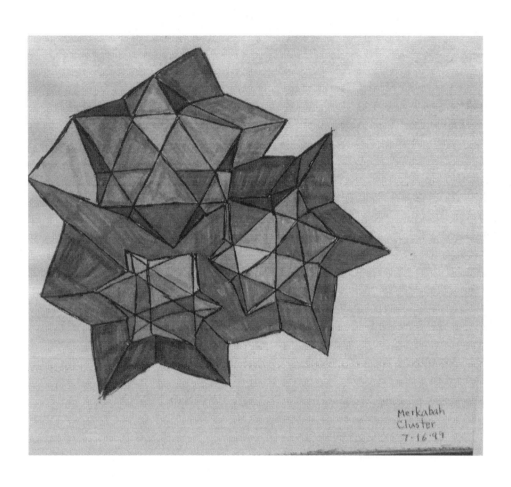

Merkabah
Cluster
7-16-97

"Meditation is a conscious vacation from concern."

"Humanity will never win a revolution against the ruling class, it is a revolution in the mind."

"SPEAK THE BEST. FORGET THE REST."

"NEWS really *means* - Nothing Ever Worth Seeing."

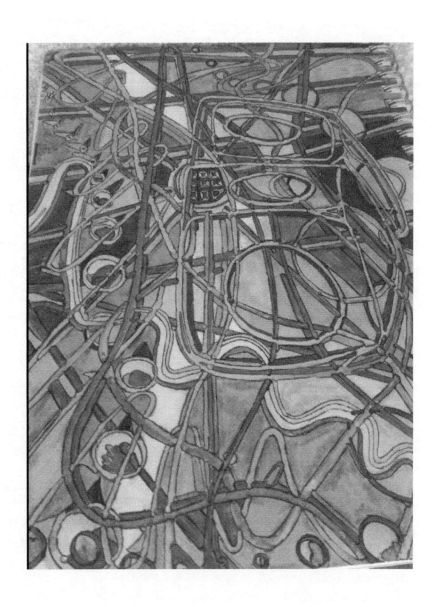

"The moment you stop questioning how good you have it, endless good appears."

EVERY STEP OF THE JOURNEY is THE JOURNEY.

"Today: May I be more conscious, courageous, loving, excited and grateful than the day before."

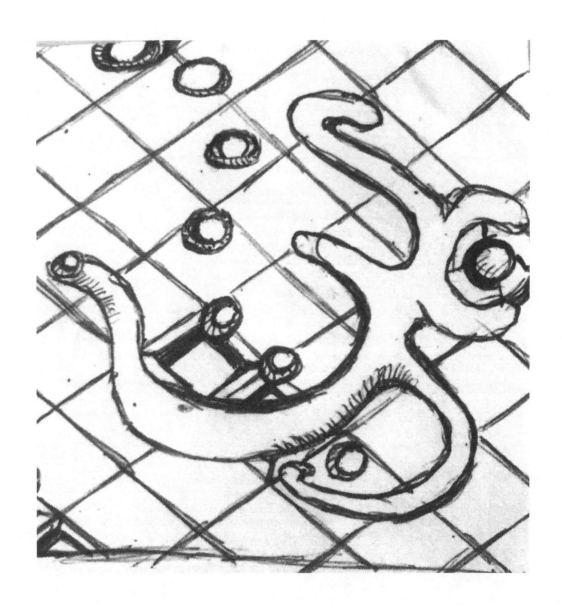

Let ♥ bring you All that You ♥. Focus on what you ♥, brings more of what you Love. Brother Sage

ABSUPPORTYOULUTELY
(c)2017
Brother Sage

HEART CROWN
12 FEB. 1980

"When one's confidence is "at an all-time high" it's best to be kneeling."

"Our hearts are calling us back to follow its guidance."

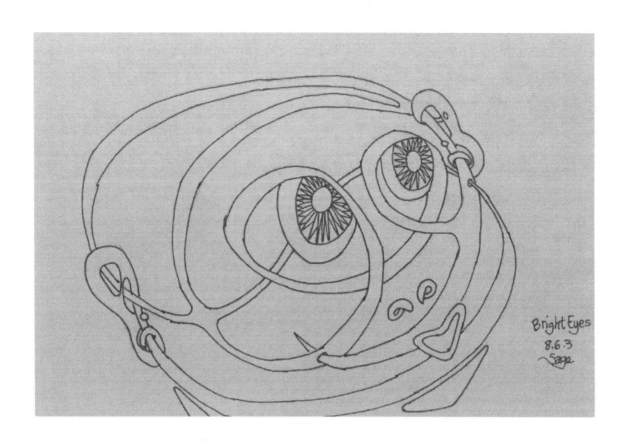

Bright Eyes
8.6.3
Sage

65

"Win back your mind and you own it and every thought that passes through it, known and unknown."

"Either get busy Loving others or get busy letting them Love you."

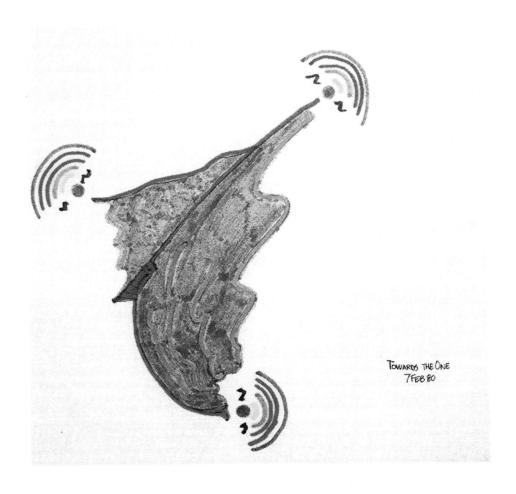

Towards the One
7 Feb 80

"When you find your path, never turn back."

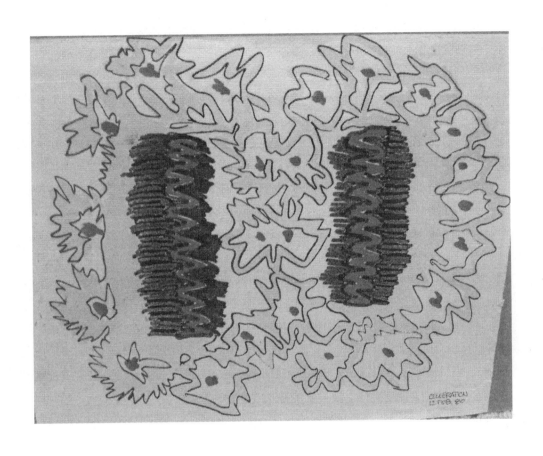

"Right now, is an International Love all, unconditionally moment. Start with yourself. Give Yourself all you got without stopping."

"Lovers are Lovers.
That's what you do.
Take it Viral. Start with You."

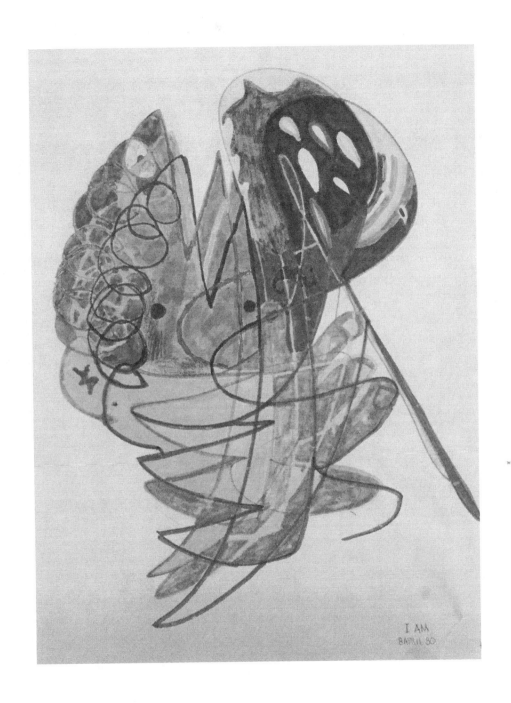

"Take this inescapable moment to wake the f*ck up. You have been resurrected."

"May all beings who still feel rejected or abandoned by their biological families remember that Divine Presence always keeps the door of its heart open for us to come home."

"Light up the world with your love! Love matters!"

om one love   4.5.11

"Love, light and oh so much laughter and giggles to you…om is where your heart is."

**Could Love be any closer
to you than it is right now?**

"Love, Money & Joy follows me everywhere like a happy puppy. I AM grateful & blessed."

"The human breath when exercized continually in an unbroken circle for an extended period of time can clear the mind/body and perpetuate a healthy, happy, long life."

© 2017 Brother Sage

"May all beings Awaken Now & return to Inescapable wholeness, balance & joy."

"Life is lived extraordinary through great humility."

"We are either sick because of what we Eat,
or because of what's eating us."

"Giving heart to hearts ends suffering."

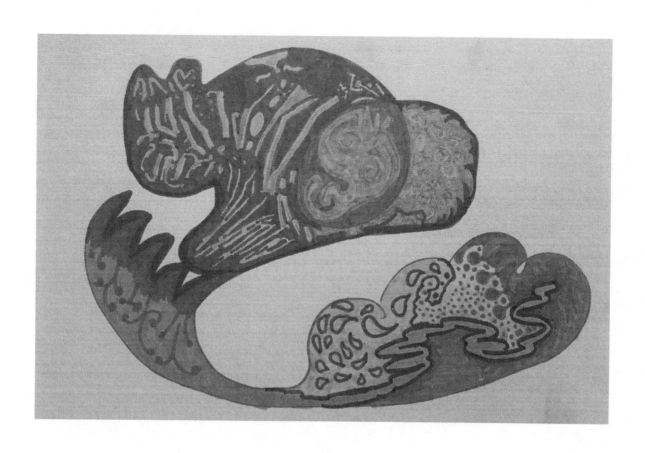

I love you cause I see the love, light & life in you & your soul. You don't have to speak, perform, or do a thing to be loved.

"Imperfection IS perfection; once you SEE it."

"I am an ongoing, ever-evolving experience & expression of Love and Light."

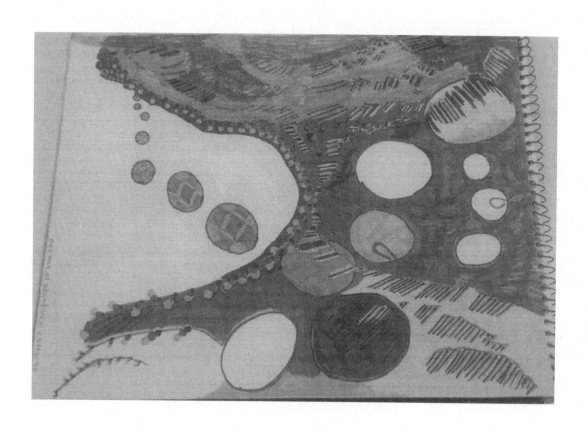

"Pay your love, dear ones, forward thru service, kindness and blessing all of life."

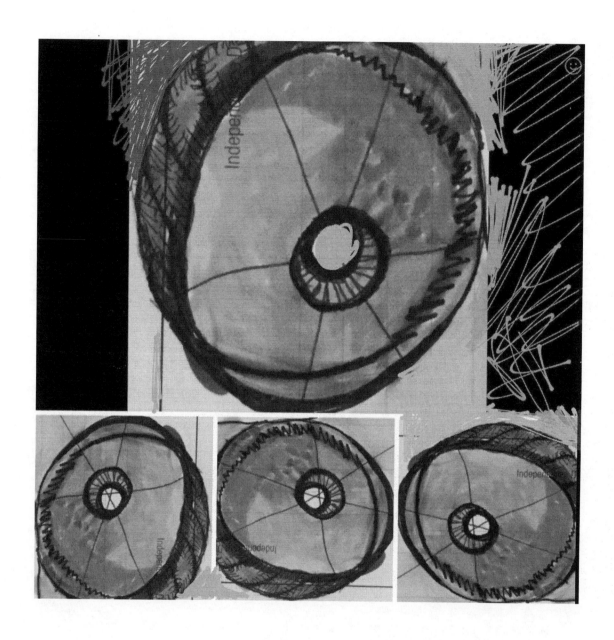

"It only takes one moment to get everything!!"

Everything up until now has happened as it did. Now what?

"Let the angels lift you (your thoughts) up."

"ABSOLOVEYOULUTELY"
© 2017 Brother Sage

"More than anything, humanity is addicted to eating."

"I live a charmed life. Miracle follows miracle. And wonders never cease."

"When you notice "where" you are "standing" or aware of how grateful you are, then you will discover your answers."

"Where will your attention, energy, and actions go in 'dis next moment? Love or Fear, One-ness or Separation, Serving or Suffering?"

Your Sacred Live Foods or Spiritual Path will not save you from your Mind.

BrotherSage.com

"My breath is my safety net."

"Sending inescapable blessings, light and energy to all beings who need it right now."

"Experience the world in this Inescapable moment through a heart centered consciousness and you will know your answers."

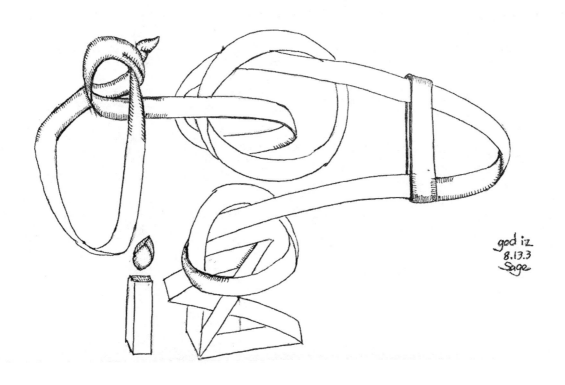

god iz
8.13.3
Sage

"Today is International "I forgive myself for everything" Day. Write this 70 times seven days and innocence returns."

I Live fully in
"the Zone Unknown" Now.
Here I AM Unguarded,
♡ Wide Open & Trusting Life.
Brother Sage

"Here's proof that Brother Sage is physically immortal: stick around a few hundred years and find out who made it."

Light up the World with your Love
Love Matters!

BrotherSage.com

"I opened up two gifts this morning: my eyes and my heart."

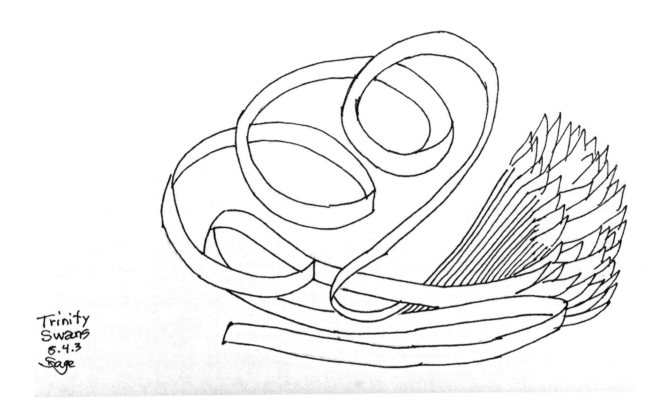

Trinity
Swans
8.4.3
Sage

117

"May all beings be blessed with health, prosperity and joy and the wisdom to keep it."

1 April 2015

"What a relief not to worry about getting enough protein, vitamins, minerals, water or any nutrients."

"Give your relationships some of your Spirit and not some of your story, see what happens."

"I'm open to the possibility of a brand-new way of looking at my life!"

"Out on a Limb"
7/20/99

"Love is my nutritional source and supply."

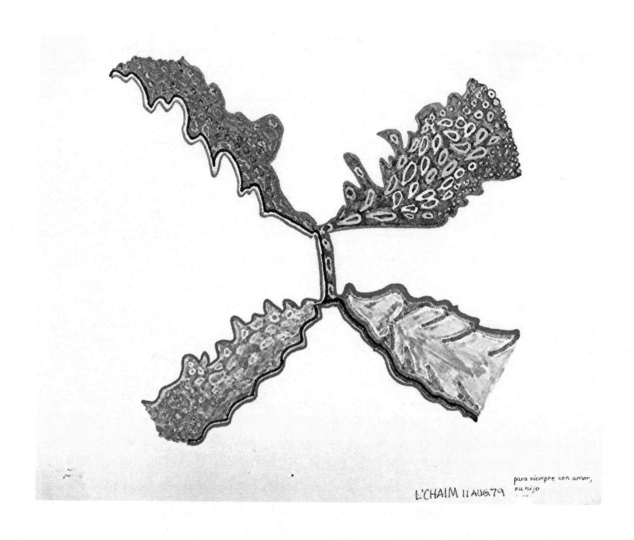

L'CHAIM 11 AUG.79   para siempre con amor,
                     su hijo

"Stay sharp, awake with an open heart. Those close to you are relying on you."

Keep single minded on Love and
Oneness and the Inescapable Life is
Yours.

BrotherSage. com

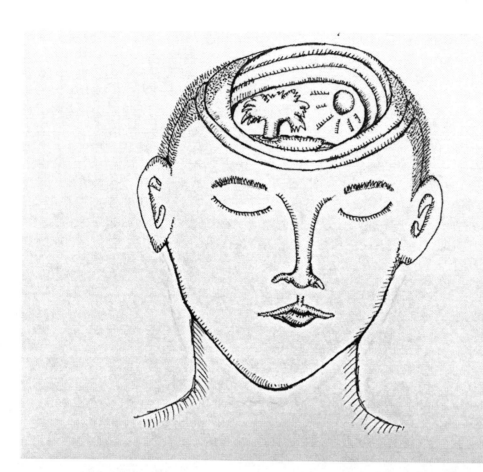

VISUALIZE A CALM PLACE
9/1/3
Sage

Endorsements:

~ "BROTHER SAGE IS ONE OF THE MOST STIMULATING THINKERS I KNOW."

In truth, simplicity, and love.

Leonard Orr, Founder of the Rebirthing Breathwork Movement

www.rebirthingbreathwork.com

~ "Brother Sage takes you to the heart of Truth. He says it so all can Hear!"
Ed and Deb Shapiro, The Unexpected Power Of Mindfulness & Meditation
edanddebshapiro.com

~ "Brother Sage sings a song of love in these beautiful quotes. How healing and uplifting to read and share these with others. His peace shines through the poetic expressions and touch my heart as they are bound to touch yours."
Peter Ragnar, Sensei, *The Longevity Sage*
www.PeterRagnar.com

~ "Colorful original art and designs. Beautiful heartfelt words. And space for YOU to add to this little book your own inspired thoughts and images. Thoughtfully creative expressions of rich inner abundance."
Udo Erasmus, *Fats That Heal Fats That Kill* and *The Book on TOTAL SEXY HEALTH*
www.udoschoice.com

~ "Let a dose of inspirational food for thought, open your mind by opening *Inescapable Quotes.*"
Brigitte Mars, Herbalist, Author and University Professor
http://www.brigittemars.com

~ "Art that exudes love, healing, stillness of mind, awareness, understanding, knowledge, optimism, peace, and enlightenment are needed today more than ever. Brother Sage's *Inescapable Quotes* offer nuggets of timeless wisdom that can retune your mental frequency toward the higher planes of existence. Love is the law of which there is no escape, and Sage's work is but a universal legal document that will advise your soul of its right to be free.
Prof. Spira, PhD, Mucusless Diet expert and author.
https://www.mucusfreelife.com

~The words of Brother Sage are expressions of empowering and inspirational energy for the soul. The Inescapable Quotes will reach your heart with truth and light. Like a blessing to all readers. Thank you for sharing these words of wisdom.

Hilde Larsen, Health and Success Coach/ Author and Keynote Speaker

https://inspiredbyhilde.com/

About the Author/Artist

Brother Sage continues to write and produce inspirational quotes, published articles like "Your Sacred Living Foods and Spiritual Path Will Not Save You from Your Mind" which appeared in Conscious Connection journal, books, videos, the coming Inescapable Book Series, talks and art since 1979. He is currently continuing a successful wellness practice of 38 years in Boulder, Colorado known as The Center of Aliveness.

www.brothersage.com

53458840R00083

Made in the USA
San Bernardino, CA
18 September 2017